BAGS OF PO[

A JUMBLE OF CLOTHES

Poems selected by Jill Bennett

Illustrated by Sue Heap

PICTURE CORGI

PICTURE CORGI BOOKS

My Body

Wherever I go, it also goes,
And when it's dressed, I'm wearing clothes.

William Jay Smith

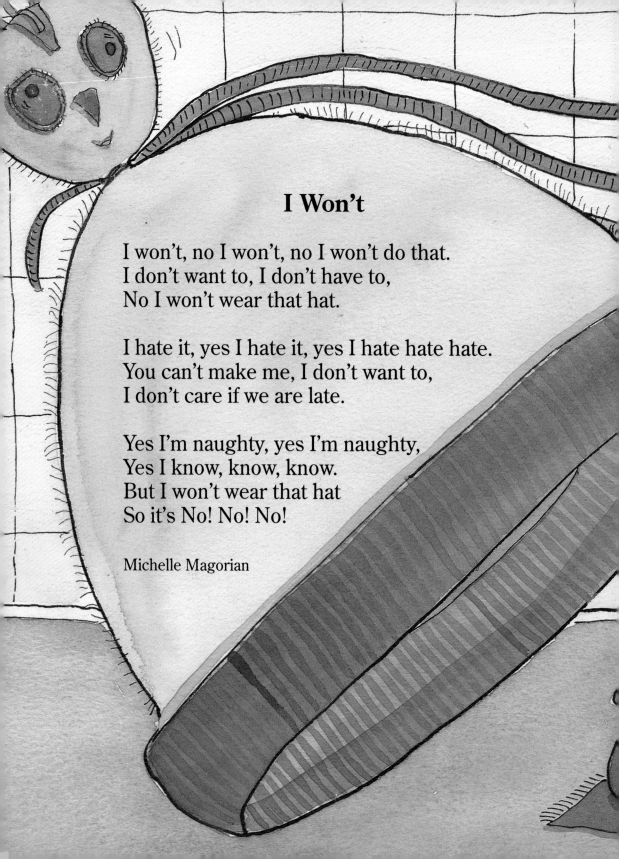

I Won't

I won't, no I won't, no I won't do that.
I don't want to, I don't have to,
No I won't wear that hat.

I hate it, yes I hate it, yes I hate hate hate.
You can't make me, I don't want to,
I don't care if we are late.

Yes I'm naughty, yes I'm naughty,
Yes I know, know, know.
But I won't wear that hat
So it's No! No! No!

Michelle Magorian

New Jacket

I've got a new jacket.
I don't even care.
What good is a jacket
You can't even wear?
  A not-everyday jacket
  That's-not-for-play jacket
  Do-as-I-say jacket
Just isn't fair.

It's yellow and red
With a zigzag design.
They bought it for me
And they said it was mine.
  A must-keep-it-neat jacket
  Not-for-the-street jacket
  Don't-you-look-sweet jacket
Isn't that fine?

I think that they bought it
Just so they could say
Go take off that jacket,
Don't wear it today.
  A don't-get-it-messed jacket
  Please-keep-it-pressed jacket
  That-is-your-best jacket
Put it away.

Mary Ann Hoberman

New Pyjamas

New pyjamas
Go bananas
Run around and shout like llamas!

New pyjarmies
Like salamis
Down our legs and up our armies!

Crisp new pyjims
Flap like pigeons
Quack like ducks and squawk like chickens!

Brand new jimjams
Just like wigwams
Yours are small and mine are a big man's!

Mark Burgess

Trainers

See me in my trainers
speeding round the house
see me in my trainers
speeding down the street
see me in my trainers
speeding to the shops.

See me in my trainers
kicking a tennis ball
see me in my trainers
kicking a hard brick wall
see me in my trainers
kicking my friend's leg.

See me in my trainers
there's a hole in my toe
see me in my trainers
the sole's worn through

you can't see me in my trainers
they're in the dustbin.

See my trainers.

Michael Rosen

My Sunday Socks

Monday morning I put rocks in my socks.
Tuesday morning I put my socks in a box.
Wednesday morning I put the box on a goat.
Thursday morning I put the goat in a coat.
Friday morning I put the coat in a tree.
Saturday morning I put the tree in the sea.
Sunday morning I put the socks on me!

Dr Fitzhugh Dodson

T-Shirt

T-shirt,
you're my best thing
though you've faded so much
no one knows what you said when you
were new.

Myra Cohn Livingston

Blue Wellies, Yellow Wellies

Blue wellies, yellow wellies,
green wellies, red.
You wear yours in puddles –
I wear mine in bed!

Judith Nicholls

Cracker Hats

Daddy looks so silly in his tissue-paper crown,
Mummy's Christmas Cracker hat looks better upside down,
Chrissie's hat is far too big and Grandma's is too small,
Mine is stuck together wrong and doesn't fit at all.
But Grandad's hat, now there's a hat! It really looks a treat,
It sits so proudly on his head, its points all sharp and neat.
Daddy says it makes him look a bit like King Canute,
At least it did until he spilled that gravy down his suit.

Jean Willis

from Idh Mubarak!

Maghrib is the name of the dusk
After the sun goes down
And Safuran is the child in the garden
Watching for the new moon.

It's here! The moon's come! It's Idh!
Idh Mubarak! she calls.

Her shalwar-zameeze is like poppies
Her dupatta scarf drifts like a breeze
Her bangles gleam as she dances
Idh Mubarak! she says.

Berlie Doherty

'Idh' is one of the main Islamic festivals
and marks the breaking of the fast at
the end of Ramadan. 'Idh Mubarak' means
'Happy Idh!'

The Magic Jumper

This morning this jumper was boring and grey
But look at the colour I've added today!
A dollop of egg yolk,
A chocolatey stripe,
A big splotch of ketchup,
Blue ink,
A BRILL-I-ANT grass stain,
A blob of black paint
And something all sticky
And pink.
This jumper is magic.
It fades back to grey overnight
And I brighten it up every day!

Sue Cowling

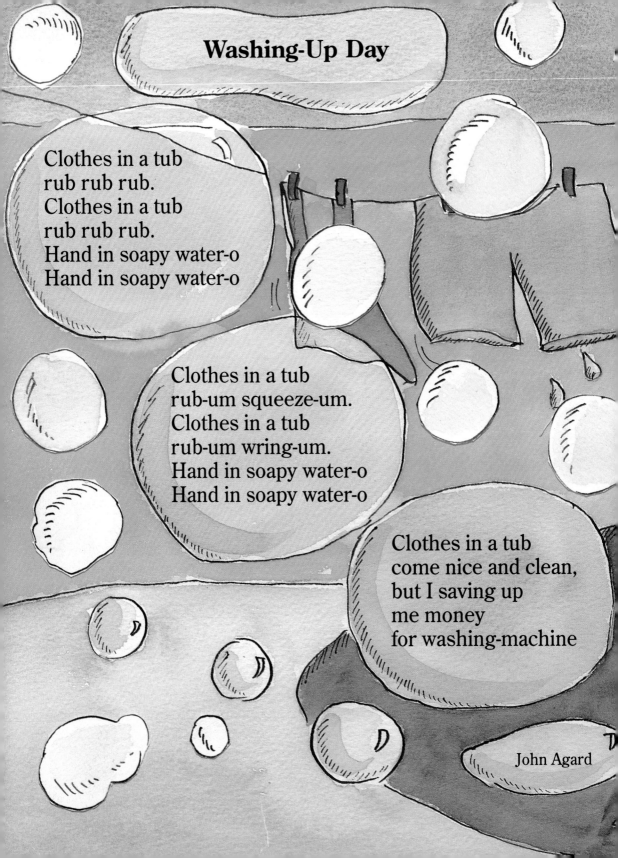

Washing-Up Day

Clothes in a tub
rub rub rub.
Clothes in a tub
rub rub rub.
Hand in soapy water-o
Hand in soapy water-o

Clothes in a tub
rub-um squeeze-um.
Clothes in a tub
rub-um wring-um.
Hand in soapy water-o
Hand in soapy water-o

Clothes in a tub
come nice and clean,
but I saving up
me money
for washing-machine

John Agard

Pssst!

Have you seen
Mrs Moggett's knickers
hanging on the line?
Long, not tiny ones,
pink ones, shiny ones,
baggy ones and dotty ones,
yellow-striped and spotty ones,
giant-sized roomy ones,
blown-up-like-balloon-y ones...
parachute-to-Paris
or take-you-to-the-moon-y ones...
Have *you* seen
Mrs Moggett's knickers
swinging on the line?

*(Pssst! Don't all shout,
but Monday's when they're out!)*

Judith Nicholls

Dufflecoat

It has four toggles made of wood,
it's warm and snug inside the hood –
but I find it very diffle-dufflecult
to do up my navy fiddle-fuddlecoat.

John Rice

Bits And Pieces

Gloves are made with fingers in
to keep out winter weather.
But socks are straight
so all the toes
are jumbled up together.
I don't know which are better off;
now which would you suppose?
It's warmer for your fingers
but much friendlier
            for toes.

Peggy Dunstan

Winter Clothes

Under my hood I have a hat
And under that
My hair is flat.
Under my coat
My sweater's blue.
My sweater's red.
I'm wearing two.
My muffler muffles to my chin
And round my neck
And then tucks in.
My gloves were knitted
By my aunts.
I've mittens too
And pants
And pants
And boots
And shoes
With socks inside.
The boots are rubber, red and wide.
And when I walk
I must not fall
Because I can't get up at all.

Karla Kuskin

In My New Clothing

In my new clothing
  I feel so different
  I must
Look like someone else.

Japanese poem by Basho
translated by Harold G. Henderson

My Dress Is Old

My dress is old, but at night the moon is kind.
Then I wear a beautiful moon-coloured dress.

American Indian (tribe unknown)

Thanks are due to the copyright holders for permission to include the following material in this collection:

John Agard, 'Washing-Up Day' from *No Hickory, No Dickory, No Dock*, published by Viking Books. ©1991 by John Agard. American Indian, 'My Dress Is Old' from *The Gift Is Rich*, published by Friendship Press. © 1951 Friendship Press. Basho, 'In My New Clothing' from *An Introduction To Haiku*, published by Doubleday. © 1958 by Basho. Mark Burgess, 'New Pyjamas' from *Can't Get To Sleep*, published by Methuen Children's Books. © 1990 by Mark Burgess. Myra Cohn Livingston, 'T-Shirt' from *O Sliver Of Liver And Other Poems*, published by Atheneum Books. © 1979 by Myra Cohn Livingston. Sue Cowling, 'The Magic Jumper'. © 1992 by Sue Cowling. Berlie Doherty, 'Idh Mubarak!' from *Let's Celebrate*, published by Oxford University Press. © 1989 by Berlie Doherty. Dr Fitzhugh Dodson, 'My Sunday Socks' from *My Red Poetry Book*, published by Thomas Nelson & Sons Ltd. © 1988 by Dr Fitzhugh Dodson. Peggy Dunstan, 'Bits And Pieces' from *In And Out The Windows*, published by Hodder and Stoughton. © 1980 by Peggy Dunstan. Mary Ann Hoberman, 'New Jacket' from *Fathers, Mothers, Sisters, Brothers*, published by Little, Brown and Co. © 1991 by Mary Ann Hoberman. Karla Kuskin, 'Winter Clothes' from *The Rose On My Cake*, published by HarperCollins Children's Books. © 1964 by Karla Kuskin. Michelle Magorian, 'I Won't' from *Waiting For My Shorts To Dry*, published by Viking Books. © 1989 by Michelle Magorian. Judith Nicholls, 'Blue Wellies, Yellow Wellies' and 'Pssst!' from *Popcorn Pie*, published by Mary Glasgow Publications. © 1988 by Judith Nicholls. John Rice, 'Dufflecoat' from *Another First Poetry Book*, published by Oxford University Press. © 1988 by John Rice. Michael Rosen, 'Trainers' from *Don't Put Mustard In The Custard*, published by André Deutsch. © 1985 by Michael Rosen. William Jay Smith, 'My Body' from *Laughing Time*, published by Little, Brown and Co. © 1955 by William Jay Smith. Jean Willis, 'Cracker Hats' from *Toffee Pockets*, published by Bodley Head. © 1992 by Jean Willis.

Every effort has been made to trace and contact copyright holders before publication. If any errors or omissions occur the publisher will be pleased to rectify these at the earliest opportunity.

Also available in the *Bags of Poems* series,
published by Picture Corgi Books

BAGS OF POEMS : FAMILY ALBUM

BAGS OF POEMS : A JUMBLE OF CLOTHES
A PICTURE CORGI BOOK : 0 552 52716 5

First published in Great Britain by Doubleday,
a division of Transworld Publishers Ltd

PRINTING HISTORY
Doubleday edition published 1993
Picture Corgi edition published 1995

Selection, arrangement and editorial matter
copyright © 1993 Jill Bennett and Doubleday Children's Books
Illustrations copyright © 1993 by Sue Heap

The right of Jill Bennett to be identified as the author of this work has been
asserted in accordance with the Copyright, Designs and Patents Act 1988.

Picture Corgi Books are published by Transworld Publishers Ltd,
61–63 Uxbridge Road, London W5 5SA, in Australia by Transworld
Publishers (Australia) Pty Ltd, 15–25 Helles Avenue, Moorebank,
NSW 2170, and in New Zealand by Transworld Publishers (NZ) Ltd,
3 William Pickering Drive, Albany, Auckland.

Printed in Belgium by Proost, Turnhout